# Human Psychology 101

## Understanding the Human Mind and What Makes People Tick

**By Alan G. Fields**

D1735214

# Table of Contents

# INTRODUCTION

From behind the bar counter, I have a great view of the whole room. It's Friday evening, and as the light outside fades, the inside of the bar turns into a fishbowl of human psychology.

The women in the window seat drink appletinis and cranberry vodkas while they elbow each other, laugh loudly, and glance over at a group of men standing on the edge of the room. They are here to play, but I can tell that they don't plan to go home with anyone; it's ladies' night out, and they're window shopping and teasing only.

The men they keep glancing at are dressed in suits and ties, but in a way that suggests that they've come straight from the office rather than going home first to put on unwrinkled shirts and evening ties. Two of them talk over each other to their buddy, who looks like he would rather be anywhere but here. I can't hear what they're saying to him, but his defeated posture and tired eyes suggest that he's recently been through a breakup, and his friends have insisted that he come out with them. He keeps checking his phone. Perhaps he expects her to call and beg him to take her back. Perhaps he's counting down the minutes until his friends will let him off the hook.

A middle-aged woman sitting to my right at the bar flirts with a twenty-something who is clearly just playing with her. Her eyes glow with a false cheer that can only come from desperation and two glasses of gin and tonic with a squeeze of lime. His eyes blink at her lazily and then scan the room again. I can almost hear his thoughts. It's still early, so he might have a chance with someone better tonight, but he doesn't want to burn his bridges with the desperate cougar, in case nothing else comes along. He's playing it safe, flirting with everyone who wanders by while maintaining enough attention on the older woman to keep her hoping.

At the other end of the bar, a couple orders a rum and coke and a whiskey, dry. The man orders his drink with a tone of careful confidence, and the woman studies the menu for a long time first. Both clearly want to make a good impression on the other. No cheap beer or frou-frou cocktails. It looks like a date, maybe a first date.

The woman keeps pushing her wavy brown hair behind her ear and licking her lips, and the man laughs a little too loudly at her story about a student in her classroom. They talk as if they know each other well. They seem to know a lot of the same people and places and have several shared memories, but going out together is not something they've done before, and it's a little awkward for both of them. After all, if this tentative relationship goes south, they'll likely still have to see each other often.

The evening wears into night, and hundreds of people come in and leave. I take orders and serve drinks from behind my counter at break-neck speed, cutting off a group of frat boys at around 9 PM and breaking up a tiff on the dance floor at around 10:30. By the time the rush has slowed enough to absorb individuals at a leisurely pace once again, the atmosphere has shifted from a frenzy of mashing bodies and clawing hands grabbing drinks from my counter to the concentrated dance party fueled by shots of fireball whiskey and Baileys with whipped cream of the after midnight crowd.

Some college kids are out on the dance floor grinding and swaying their hips. The girls are in a complicated choreography of wanting to be noticed by the guys but not wanting to be too noticed by the wrong ones. They'll play with the ugly guy, but they dance back to their friend group clusters as soon as they've gotten his attention. Several of the guys have had enough to drink that they are losing a grasp on what no means.

"I said hands off," a pretty brunette snaps at a tattooed guy with a Mohawk who keeps trying to grab her ass and laughing at her objections.

"You know you like it," he slurs. From my place behind the bar I see the gleam in his eye. I would like to believe that it's the alcohol talking, but in my experience, a man who will disrespect a woman when he's drunk, would probably do so sober as well.

His buddy with a line of lip piercings laughs loudly, but it sounds fake. He's uncomfortable with the situation. "Let's get out of this joint," he says. "There's that place up the street we haven't been to yet."

Mohawk considers this. His buddy has just offered him a way to save face with the brunette and all of the people watching. He glares at the brunette. "Chicks are probably hotter there," he says, and he leads his buddies out.

Meanwhile, I've had to cut off the cougar at the bar, and she's still sitting there, nursing a water and the blind hope that the guy hitting on her and stringing her along earlier will come back and take her home with him, even though he left the bar an hour ago.

Even on a tame Friday night like tonight, the complexity of the human mind is still evident in the throngs of people around me. As a bartender, I am both center stage and invisible. It's the perfect looking glass into the human condition, into what they want, dread, hope, and fear. Learning what makes people tick has always fascinated me, and my stint as a bartender has given me a real interest in psychology that I wish to pass along to anyone who's interested.

*What's In This Book?*

This book is meant to show you all the facets of a human being and how they work together to make a person tick. It's not a psychological treatise or a DSM-V. It's a collection of my own research of psychology and stories from my life and those of my friends and acquaintances that help illustrate the principles I'm going to be telling you about.

I will be dividing this book into seven aspects of human psychology: emotions, personality, decision-making, morality, perception, behavior, and relationships.

Understanding the human mind is a complicated array of wirings of the past combined with the physical and chemical inclinations of the present. Psychology is the study of the human brain, but it's so much more than a mere dissection of the gooey gray mass trapped in our skulls; it's a study of what makes us tick as individuals and as a species.

To understand what makes someone tick is to have mastered a sort of psychological sleight of hand, and I hope that this book serves as a useful step on your way to mastery over that brand of magic trick. How human beings think and behave is an unendingly fascinating study, one that reveals how simple and elegant and, on the other hand, complex and mysterious we are.

# CHAPTER ONE: PSYCHOLOGY OF EMOTIONS

What is the first thing you notice about someone? Their last season Prada heels? Their teal sweater vest? The size of their muscles? Their bra size? Eye color? Height? These can provide important insights into a person's mind, but alone, they don't tell us nearly as much as a person's emotions. As a bartender, I often find that I look past the outfit and am much more fascinated by the emotions people display.

The beauty of emotions is that they are, more or less, universal. Fear and happiness look the same on virtually all human faces.

In an evolutionary sense, emotions are meant to heighten our survival. When you lose your child in the grocery store, your heart pounds and your senses become more sharp and focused on the one most important task at hand: finding your kid. All other things fall by the wayside. You don't notice the hot cashier or the sale on granola bars. Psychologists disagree about whether the physiological response comes first or whether the emotion comes first, but to be honest, it's a bit of a chicken or egg argument, especially in terms of reading people.

You don't always have the opportunity to hook a person up to heart rate monitors or feel a pulse while you study a person's face for emotional responses. Therefore, your key to understanding how people tick is in watching their face for an emotional reaction, however brief it may be.

Emotions are like a psychological interface that we use to determine if we think someone likes us, if we should approach someone, when we should present a certain argument, and when we need to back away. They also heighten our perception of a situation. This is true for you and me, and it is true for every person you will ever meet. Understanding this is one of the key factors in learning how a person ticks.

Holing up in a dark room, eating a mountain of chocolate and ice cream, and watching romantic comedies while sobbing and refusing to brush your teeth might sound like irrational behavior until you understand that the woman in question has just been jilted at the alter by a man she believed loved her with all his heart. When you understand the range of human emotions, you have a database of possible explanations for behavior, attitudes, and perception.

The middle-aged woman at the end of the bar might perceive me as some sort of hero because, in the face of her depression, I am the one who pours the gin that numbs her distress over her showing age, her recent divorce, and her fear that she won't make anything of herself at all.

Mirror neurons provide a gateway from one person to another. I can understand how you feel by looking at you and noting your facial expression and your posture. Our brains are designed to relate to others, which is what make emotions a great place to start in learning to understand the human mind.

### *Reading Microexpressions*

According to research by Dr. Paul Ekman, a psychologist who helped to pioneer the study of emotions and facial expressions, microexpressions are the most accurate means of figuring out how people really feel about any given thing. Microexpressions are defined as facial expressions lasting for a fraction of a second that either deliberately or unconsciously conceal a true emotion. They are very difficult to fake, which makes them exceedingly useful, perhaps even more so than a polygraph test (Ekman, 2016).

The range of human emotion can be broken down into seven groups: happiness, sadness, anger, surprise, fear, disgust, and contempt. Most facial expressions exist in variations of these seven emotions. Being able to recognize these in the people around you is a giant leap toward understanding how people tick.

By learning to read microexpressions, you will gain valuable insight into what people are really feeling, when they are telling the truth, when they are lying, and what makes them tick.

*Happiness*

Spread the corners of your lips up and back. You cheeks will rise. A wrinkle will run from the edge of your nose to the outer edge of your mouth. Your eyes will crinkle at the corners. Your lower eyelid may be tense or wrinkled. Real happiness will have all of these characteristics.

People fake happiness all the time. At the bar where I work, I watch women trying to turn heads by laughing often at what their friends are saying, but though their mouths are stretched wide, and all of their teeth are showing, I can see by the lack of crows feet at the corners of their eyes that it's a mask.

A fake smile is a yearbook photo; a real smile is a moment of completely forgetting what your face is supposed to look like and feeling genuinely happy.


*Sadness*

Draw the inside corners of your eyebrows together and up. Pull the corners of your lips down. Bring your jaw up and push your lower lip out. This is what sadness looks like, and it's the hardest microexpression to fake.

I went to a funeral once for an old college professor. He'd been a nasty old man, and most of us went because we were in his class that semester and we'd been told that there would be free food. We all knew what it looked like to feel sad, and we put on our best sad faces, but I would bet anything that our microexpressions were giving us away as the gleeful, hungry liars that we were.

Meanwhile, it was interesting to note that the daughter of the deceased, who was putting on a smile for all of the guests and graciously accepting hugs and handshakes, looked truly desolate beneath her show of bravado. It was real sadness that one who does not feel it cannot hope to mimic.

*Anger*

Lower your eyebrows and pull them together. Vertical lines will appear between your brows, and your lower lid will tense. Press your lips together firmly, and jut your chin out. Your nostrils may dilate, and your eyes may bulge or stare hard. This is what anger looks like.

For a few months I dated a woman who never seemed to get angry with me, even when I was doing things that I knew she had to find irritating. She never raised her voice or threatened to break up with me. At first, I thought she was just super chill. Then after three months, it began to strike me as strange that we never fought or disagreed about anything. When I asked her about this, she shrugged it off and said that she just thought it was a waste of time to get angry.

I let this go at first. I was apparently lucky. Then, as I got to know her better and learned the difference between what she liked and only pretended to like, I became more curious about whether she truly never got angry or whether she simply chose to hide her anger from me. I brought up the subject of politics one day, which I'd noticed she didn't seem to like, as she tended to steer political discussions in another direction as quickly as possible.

Curious, and feeling a little sadistic, I refused to let her change the course of the conversation to something innocuous like plants or floor tiles. I said the most inflammatory statements I could think of, and after pushing the subject on her for several minutes without giving in, I finally caught a fleeting glimpse of anger in her face, which she quickly masked. It was only a glimpse, but it was all I needed to know that there were probably plenty of things about me that made her angry that she kept hidden from me.

I'm not saying you should go around trying to make people angry so that you know what it looks like. I'm just saying that when a person is angry, there's only so much of their anger they will be able to hide. Their face will eventually betray them, whether they realize it or not.

*Surprise*

Raise your eyebrows so that they are curved, stretching the skin beneath them taut. Drop your jaw and part your teeth. Horizontal wrinkles will traverse your forehead. Your eyelids will be open, and, often, the whites of your eyes will show above and below your irises. This is what surprise looks like.

When my sister, who was seventeen at the time, told my parents she was pregnant, I watched my mother's face struggle between flashes of happiness and anger. My father's face flashed surprise and then was masked with anger and contempt. I realized, watching my parents, that our mom had already known she was pregnant.

"When is your next doctor appointment?" Mom asked, quietly.

Our dad seethed while visibly trying to keep his temper in check.

My sister told them.

"I'll go with you," Mom said. "When are you due?"

"Who is the son of a bitch who did this to you?" Dad said.

My sister was quiet as sadness and contained anger flashed forward and disappeared. "He told me to get an abortion, so I told him to never talk to me again."

I could tell by the control in her voice and on her face that it had been a hard decision. She had believed herself to be in love with her boyfriend, but he apparently hadn't loved her enough to want to help her raise their child. I could imagine the surprise coloring her face to hear him tell her to abort the baby. Clearly, he didn't know my sister as well as he thought he did.


*Fear*

Raise your eyebrows and draw them together. Raise your upper eyelids and tense your lower ones, drawing them up a little. Part your mouth, tense your lips, and draw them back. White will show above your eye but not below it. Wrinkles will appear vertically between your eyes rather than just horizontally at the top of your forehead.

I still bartend sometimes on the weekends, but now I'm a business analyst in a corporate headquarters. A few weeks ago, my boss called us all into a conference room to tell us about a really bad error one of us had made that had cost the company hundreds of thousands of dollars. As the boss waxed eloquent about the seriousness of the mistake and assured us that he would find the culprit and fire him, I looked around the room at the faces of my coworkers. Nearly all of them looked surprised and concerned. One man, who at first looked like he was surprised and concerned with the rest, showed flashes of fear.

In this circumstance, I could think of no reason why anyone in the room should be afraid unless they were the one who made the error. After a thorough investigation, the boss found the man who had made the lethal error; it was indeed the man who had showed fear while we were in the conference room.

*Disgust*

Raise your upper lip. Draw the insides of your eyebrows down. Raise your cheeks and wrinkle your nose. Lines will appear below your bottom eyelids. This is the expression you make when you smell something bad or when someone or something disgusts you.

A while back, I was at a housewarming party for some friends with a lot of people I didn't know that well. I was talking to one woman about her work in an animal hospital. Eventually, she asked me what I do for a living. I told her I was a bartender, because even though I had a day job in a cubicle, a lot of women thought bartending sounded way cooler. They knew what that was and felt more at ease with me when they could find some way to relate to me.

Then I watched her upper lip move up and the lines appear below her bottom eyelids for the briefest of moments. She covered quickly, smiling and nodding and excusing herself to find something else to drink. Her disgust didn't give me a full explanation of her thoughts or anything, but I guessed, and had my friends whose party it was corroborate, that she was husband hunting and was only looking for a man with a "real" job. She considered bartending to be something a twenty-two-year-old kid would do to seem cool to his buddies and pick up chicks, not something a guy in his thirties would do because he just liked it.

*Contempt*

Raise one side of your mouth, and that's contempt. It can be one of the easiest expressions to mask with a quick smile or whatever the more appropriate expression would be.

Dr. John Gottman, a psychologist who has studied and written about marriage and relationships for many years, says that the number one predictor of relationship failure is the presence of contempt. Contempt stems from a lack of respect and a feeling that the other person is inferior. It often manifests itself in sarcasm and cynicism.

I've watched many of my married friends argue and fight, and Dr. Gottman's research seems to coincide with my own experience. Two of my friends would argue by lobbing sarcastic comments back and forth in a display of truly troubling contempt for each other. Their microexpressions—and I dare say there regular expressions much of the time—matched their tones. Within two years, they were signing divorce papers and parting ways bitter, spent, and certain that the other was entirely to blame for their failed marriage.

While microexpressions are indicative of a person's true feelings in any given situation, it's often a lot harder to figure out the reasons behind the expression. It could be very straightforward, or the situation could be more complex than you assume. Maybe the coworker concealing fear at being accused of fraud is afraid because he's the one who did it, or maybe he's afraid because he knows who did it, and he deeply cares about that person and warned them not to.

People are complex, and there are usually many possibilities for why people are feeling a certain emotion. Be careful not to jump to unfair conclusions or make accusations until you allow a proper explanation from the person or have further evidence to verify your story. Many factors play into emotions. People with different personalities may be prone to feeling different emotions in the same circumstances, and that's what the next chapter is meant to address: personalities.

# CHAPTER TWO: PSYCHOLOGY OF PERSONALITY

As a bartender, I've noticed the seeming correlation between the sorts of drinks people order and their apparent personality. If a guy orders Miller Lite, it's because he's cheap or poor and wants to get laid. If a dude orders a White Zinfindel, he's probably gay. When a woman comes in and orders a blended cocktail, it's easy to jump to the conclusion that she's whiny, flaky, and high maintenance. Sadly, these stereotypes often live up to their reputations, at least for that particular moment in time, which is why it's so easy to return to them when we need to quickly size someone up.

Stereotypes exist for a reason, but personality goes much deeper than a stereotype based on a drink order at the bar. I myself can go for some good old fashioned boxed white zin on an off night, and I am neither gay nor a clueless girl at the bar for the first time.

What does this prove? Merely that personality is made up of numerous other factors that often live below the surface in any given situation. So many variables come together to form certain personality types that it's frequent that two people can have similar personalities and come from completely different life experiences, or two people can come from the same life experience, twins or close siblings for example, and have completely different personalities.

Often we think of personality as something that is fixed, something that is a constant in all circumstances that determines how a person will react in any given situation. But the truth is that personality is like a living body of water: consisting of the same elements most of the time but continually being mixed and tossed by storms, currents, and relationships with other bodies of water.

A Myers-Briggs test, one of the most popular personality tests currently available, will provide an accurate explanation only up to a point. Perhaps a person's personality type, according to the test, says that they are a nurturer and are constantly looking for ways to help others become better versions of themselves. For the most part, this description might be fairly accurate, but what about those times when the nurturer is emotionally drained? They might feel resentment when someone asks them for help they would normally jump at the chance to give. What if they're going through a bad breakup with an abusive partner? They might feel that all of their nurturing skills have been a total waste and isolate themselves from others.

Personalities are equal parts stable and in flux. A personality test can describe natural tendencies, but a lot of variables will be at play in any given situation. The rest of this chapter will explore different personality types with the objective of giving you insight into how each one ticks.

## *Main Personality Types and How They Tick*

In this section, I'm going to use the categories from the Myers-Briggs personality test to explain how different personalities work. I'm choosing to use this set of traits over other personality test styles because in talking with various people in my life, this was the test that people seemed to know the most about. In fact, many of my friends and acquaintances have taken a version of the Myers-Briggs test and could proudly state their personality type and description, even if they didn't understand how the entire system works.

In this chapter, my goal is to give you a baseline of understanding how the different traits compare with each other.

Since traits all exist on a continuum, I'll talk about each trait as it relates to its opposite trait. Because these traits are on a continuum, don't get sucked into the idea that a person has to be either one or the other. This would create a false dichotomy. A person is hardly ever all the way to one side or all the way to the other, but a mix of the two, with one usually being more dominant.

*Introversion (I) or Extraversion (E)*

Whether a person is more introverted or more extroverted depends on how they prefer to focus on the world. An introvert will tend to focus on their own internal world, the thought-scape of their own mind. An extrovert prefers to focus on the external world.

While an introvert will gain energy from having alone time to contemplate ideas or pictures or sift through memories, an extrovert will gain energy from being around people, interacting with the world outside of themselves, and having many different hobbies and activities that they enjoy. An extrovert tends to be more inclined to jump into an activity or job and make things happen, while an introvert will think about something until they have examined all of the angles and have come to a level of certainty about what they plan to do.

Understanding the difference between these two traits will give you insight into how a person ticks when they say, "I'm an introvert," or "I'm an extrovert."

Introversion is not the same as shyness or reclusiveness. In fact, a person who ranks highly on introversion can still want to seek out new experiences and be the life of the party. The opposite is also true; a person who ranks highly in extroversion can sometimes want to be alone to contemplate ideas and memories and bask in the quiet.

*Intuition (N) or Sensing (S)*

This category refers to the information a person takes in. A sensing person will focus on the basic information, while a person who uses intuition will prefer to interpret that information and find or add meaning to it.

A sensing person tends to look at the facts that are gathered through the five senses and see the bottom line. They learn best when they can see the practical use of something and have less use for symbols and words. While they tend to be more down-to-earth and see things as they are, they also can completely miss opportunities for innovation and better solutions.

A person who uses more intuition will tend to focus more on an impression or a feeling of a situation rather than on what they can hear, see, touch, taste, and smell. They like to read between the lines to draw out meanings that can't always be gleaned from the senses. They are constantly looking for meanings and new ideas, and in the process, they can sometimes neglect to think about how to make their innovative ideas a reality.

These traits are good to pay close attention to when you are working on a project with another person or group of people. Noting who is throwing out the facts and who is throwing out the interesting ideas can clue you in on how the various members of your group think and help you talk to them in ways that show that you value their strengths and still move the project in the direction that it needs to go.

*Thinking (T) or Feeling (F)*

In decision-making, a person on the thinking end of the continuum will look at the situation with logic and consistency, while a person on the feeling end of the continuum will look at the people and try to see and understand any special circumstances that are at play.

Don't confuse thinking with intelligence or feeling with emotion. Everyone experiences emotion and uses their intelligence in decision-making; these are different from the thinking and feeling traits.

A thinking person seeks to not let their personal opinions and others' personal opinions influence their decisions. They will look for a logical explanation in a situation that seems inconsistent with others like it, and they will be more truthful than tactful. They are often seen as cool, detached decision-makers who are very task-oriented. People who are more on the feeling end of the continuum often perceive them as cold or indifferent.

A feeling person tends to take into account the thoughts and feelings of all people involved in a decision and seek to make a decision that promotes the most group harmony. This person gets nervous or uncomfortable when others are unhappy and will seek to find a compromise that will make the most people happy. Their weakness tends to be that in the midst of taking everyone's thoughts and opinions into account, they miss the cold, hard facts of a situation and sometimes come off as being too subjective or idealistic.

*Judging (J) or Perceiving (P)*

The judging or perceiving continuum refers to how a person tends to feel about structure in their life and how they interact in the outside world. A judging person will prefer a more rigid structure and will work to nail down that structure as soon as they can. A perceiving person likes to stay open to possibilities.

This last continuum is a little bit more complicated to explain than the others, because it's not merely about whether a person likes structure or not; it's about how they tend to appear to the outside world. A person who tends to interact with the outside world when they are making decisions, will appear to be very structured, organized, and orderly to others. A person who tends to interact with the outside world by taking in information will appear to others to be more spontaneous and adaptable.

A judging person interacts with the outer world using their decision-making trait (whether that is through thinking or feeling). This person likes to make decisions and stick to them. This person will make plans or lists, will work before playing, and will seem, to others, to be very organized and task-oriented. Since this trait applies to how they prefer to act in the outside world, that doesn't mean that these things are true of them internally. They might still feel that they are very flexible and open to new ideas and spontaneity. Do not confuse the judging trait with being judgmental, as they are not related to each other.

A perceiving person interacts with the outer world using their information trait (whether that is through sensing or intuition). This person will seek to take in more information rather than making a decision, which causes others to see them as spontaneous and flexible.

They prefer to understand information as opposed to organizing it. They often mix their work with their play, work with bursts of energy, and are spurred to productivity by approaching deadlines. While this person appears to be unorganized or completely spontaneous, they often feel very decisive and that they stick to their plans and routines. Do not confuse the perceiving trait with being perceptive, as they are not the same thing.

Understanding the nuances of these traits will give you insight into how people relate externally with the world around them, which can, in turn, help you better understand how they tick.

## What To Do With These Personality Types

When a stranger at the grocery store pisses you off, you have the option of walking away and ranting about the annoying person to your friends or spouse and never having to see that person again. You don't ask them about their personality type to try to determine if they meant to offend you by informing you that your favorite breakfast cereal has a lot of high fructose corn syrup in it or if they were just trying to help you out, because they believe that you must not know the facts or you wouldn't be buying it.

However, with your family members, friends, and colleagues, walking away forever, talking shit, and never seeing them again isn't necessarily an option, and often you have something to lose by cutting ties with these people. That's when understanding their personalities can be most helpful in helping you to understand how they tick and more peacefully resolve conflicts and communicate your thoughts in a way they will understand.

For example, you might have a really interesting business idea that you think has the propensity to revolutionize the entire fitness community, and you want to pitch it to your buddy in marketing to see if he'll help you out.

Maybe you're most excited about the groundbreaking nature of this project and about helping people reach their fitness goals more easily than ever before, but you know that your buddy is very fact-based and logical. He appreciates innovation only insofar as it has a large enough target audience to be profitable.

How do you pitch your idea to him? You need to speak in a language that he will find most persuasive. Do your research and figure out what the target audience is, whether there's a need for your product, and how much money you could make. If your idea is as good as you say it is, let the facts speak for themselves, as these are what will persuade you friend over any pretty rhetoric about building a better future.

Here's another example. My buddy and his wife were in constant conflict over when the housework should get done. He wanted to work in spurts and take frequent breaks to watch a TV show or make a nice meal. She wanted to get it all done in one swift cleaning binge and have the rest of the day to hang out and relax. I was able to point out to my buddy that his wife wasn't trying to be a drill sergeant; she was just more of a sensing, thinking, judging sort of person, and he was more of an intuition feeling, perceiving sort of person. Neither of them were wrong; they just had different preferences.

Once they realized this, they were able to decide on a compromise regarding the housework that made room for and validated both of their preferences. When they needed to get a lot of chores done in a short period of time, like before company came over, they used her method, but they agreed to always take a meal break at the appropriate meal hour. When they just had a few things to get done in no specific time frame, they used his method but agreed that they would see the specific task to completion before taking a break. This way, both of them could feel productive, and the housework no longer had to be a huge sore spot between them.

Not all conflicts will be that straightforward, but sometimes just knowing the difference between something that is better or worse versus something that is just different from what you want can help you walk a mile in another's shoes and, if not agree, then at least understand where they're coming from.

# CHAPTER THREE: PSYCHOLOGY OF DECISION-MAKING AND IMPULSES

While I was bartending one Saturday night, I watched as a somewhat inebriated guy walked up to a woman, complimented her, and offered her a backhanded compliment that went something like, "Why does it seem like all of the beautiful women are too prudish to be good in bed?" Then, after a few minutes of chatting with her, he invited her home with him. She adamantly refused and looked completely insulted that he would ask her such a thing after a five-minute acquaintance. He then walked up to another woman and did the same thing. She accepted, and they left the bar together, hand in hand.

Had he taken the time to read his audience, he might have noticed that the first woman he asked to go home with him showed contempt the moment he gave her the backhanded compliment. Had he noticed that, he could have spared himself the embarrassment of being rejected so soundly in front of all of the people around him at the bar. The second woman, on the other hand, showed momentary surprise and then spent the next few minutes trying to convince him that she wasn't like most women he met, because she was very good in bed. When he asked her home with him, she took this as an invitation to prove it to him that she was as good as she claimed to be.

Same guy, same tactic, very different decisions. Why is that? This chapter will explore the different factors that go into the decision-making process that make it turn out so drastically different for everyone. Understanding the psychology of how decision-making works and what considerations different people place more importance on will help you gain a clearer picture of how they tick.

### *Factors In Decision-Making*

There isn't one distinct decision-making process that all people follow. Not only are people different from each other, but decisions themselves are different from one to the next and require different processes depending on the decision that needs to be made. Some decisions, like whether to press snooze or have ten more minutes in the shower is a low-stakes decision that many of us make in a matter of milliseconds.

*Gravity*

When I'm deciding what to wear on my day off for going to the gym and running some errands, I'll grab the first non office clothing my hands touch and put them on. The whole decision-making process on these days takes about three seconds and consists of very little, if any, cognitive stress. I don't feel the need to make a pros and cons list or figure out if I look better in blue or green or consult my database of past experiences to determine which outfit made me feel the most successful. Since my primary objective on a normal day off is to be comfortable, the gravity of my decision on what to wear is very low.

On the other hand, if I'm going on a very promising first date with a beautiful and funny woman I met at a party thrown by a mutual friend, I might try on several color combinations, labor over whether I should wear a suit or play it more casual, call up a buddy to get advice, go on the internet to look up "what to wear on first date", freak out because I realize that most of the articles online are written for a female audience, put on the first combination I tried, and strike some power poses in the mirror to solidify my decision. Because the outcome of this evening is important to me, and I feel that my decision on what to wear might, in some way, ruin my chance with the perfect woman, the decision has a lot more gravity.

The amount of gravity the decision holds will determine, in part, the process you use to make a decision. An important decision will consist of more serious thought than one that a person perceives doesn't really matter. You can often tell how important a decision is to someone based on how they are approaching it.

If Jenny is spending more of her time stressing over which table runners and centerpieces to have at her wedding reception than she is about writing her vows or discussing with her husband to be what it will mean to be married, then you might have just gained some valuable insight into Jenny's personality and the mentality with which she is entering into her marriage. Perhaps in Jenny's mind, a perfect wedding will equal a perfect marriage.

You can tell a lot about how a person ticks by paying attention to what decisions stress them out and what decisions they make flippantly. Don't assume, however, that just because a person acts impulsively that the decision must not have much gravity or that just because they are stressing over something that it must be a matter of life or death. People, in their complexity, will surprise you.

*Past Experience*

People learn from the past. My friend, Charlotte, has a knack for dating men who are bad for her. She's been with liars, cheaters, assholes, dicks, and dudes with commitment problems. What's worse is that she usually knows what she's getting herself into when she's with these types of men.

"Then why do you keep making the same mistakes?" I asked her once. "Isn't that the definition of insanity?"

She laughed a little and then thought about it for a moment. "I guess it's just familiar. I know what to expect from them, and when the worst happens, I know I can deal with it. What happens if I'm with someone who seems like a really good person and then he lets me down? I don't know if I can handle that, because I've never dated one of the good guys."

She made an interesting point. Past experiences are psychological factors in decision-making, but they don't always work in the way you assume they will.

A person's decision on how to raise their children will probably stem, in part, from how their parents raised them. However, for some people, that means doing exactly what their parents did, and for others it means doing the opposite of what their parents did.

In financial decision-making, the most successful people tend to make decisions that don't take into account past wins and losses and only examine the facts that are in play for that specific decision (Juliusson et al., 2005).

Outliers aside, overall, studies show that people tend to avoid making the same decisions that resulted in a negative experience and repeat past decisions that resulted in a positive experience. For example, when a person decides to cheat on their income taxes and gets busted for income tax evasion, he is probably a lot less likely to make the decision to cheat on the forms again. On the other hand, if a husband cleans the house while his wife is at work, and she has sex with him as soon as she sees all the work he's done, he might feel like cleaning the house is something he should do more often.

## Cognitive Biases

Cognitive biases are patterns of thought that are based on faulty logic, inaccurate data, generalizations, or an error in memory.

A belief bias might cause one to rely overly much on prior knowledge and beliefs when coming to a decision about something. Rather than looking at the logic of a specific argument being made, a person might ignore a poorly made argument if they agree with the conclusion.

My friend, Jude, is very much in favor of having the right to bear arms. He loves guns, owns several, and has a list of very well thought out reasons for why they shouldn't be taken away by the government. However, whenever a fellow gun enthusiast tries to make his case by saying things like, "Guns aren't dangerous," and, "You can't feel safe without a gun," he gets angry. "We might agree on the fact that we think we should be allowed to keep our guns," he says, "but I don't agree with his reasons. Guns are dangerous and should be respected. That's why we don't want the government to take them away and stockpile them."

In a hindsight bias, a person might look at an event after the fact and make the judgment call that the results of the event were, in fact, inevitable, whether they were or not. For example, if a surgeon is being prosecuted for negligently causing the death of a patient during a complicated, high-risk surgery, the prosecutor might go through the operation and the patient's condition and records in vivid detail and conclude from evidence after the fact that the surgeon should have known that this would happen and not taken the risk, even though it was the patient's decision to try it, and he was fairly warned of the risk involved.

An omission bias might cause someone to judge an action to be worse or more harmful than an equally harmful or wrong omission. Some psychologists question whether this bias truly represents an error in thinking or if there is any real moral distinction between doing something bad and allowing something bad to happen. Parents might decide not to vaccinate a child, because they have heard that some children have died from vaccinations. However, they forget that the disease being vaccinated against is much more likely to kill their child than the vaccine itself.

I will say more on the moral implications of the omission bias in the next chapter, but here it's important to note that some people will make decisions based on how they view the difference between doing bad and allowing bad.

A confirmation bias occurs when people see an event and only observe the things that they expect to happen. If a person goes to a family reunion expecting that all of their extended family members are judging them for being an exotic dancer, then she'll make different decisions in terms of her behavior toward her relatives than if she goes to the reunion with the idea that no one cares about her job.

*Socioeconomic Class*

It's fairly well known that socioeconomic class has an impact on cognitive development. Maslow's hierarchy of needs shows the order in which needs must be met in order to advance to the next level of the hierarchy. People who are living in poverty are often constantly lacking one or more of the foundational human needs, and are therefore less likely to advance to levels of self-fulfillment and actualization.

A person who is living on the brink of starvation or exhausted from the hours of factory work required of them to pay their bills and clothe their children is far less likely to carve out time and money to get an education or think deeply about philosophy. Their mind is on survival, and the decisions they make are toward that end.

Additionally, people in a low socioeconomic class may have access to fewer resources that might aid or educate them, which might lead to them being unable to make informed decisions about things. When things happen that are beyond their control, they won't have the connections, resources, or knowledge to fight against oppression or bad circumstances.

A person living in great wealth or even in a moderate financial state, on the other hand, has the luxury of making decisions based on what they want rather than on what they need.

They can choose to take a day off work to golf at the club or go shopping, because they don't have to worry about where their next meal is coming from.

For the year after graduating from high school, I took a year off from school and struck out on my own to take the world by storm. Coming from a middle class family, I believed that anything was possible if I just tried hard enough, so I started my own business. I'd never had to think much about money before, and I applied the same thoughtless mentality to my business, which struggled on for seven months until my landlord threatened to evict me from my apartment, the only food in my fridge was ketchup and a can of beans, and the only furniture I hadn't sold to buy groceries was my mattress.

Hungry, broke, and exhausted from worry about my eviction notice, I swallowed my pride, moved back in with my parents, and decided to go to bartending school so I could have a skill that would make me money wherever I ended up.

The standard of life a person is used to can color the way they see the world, and, in turn, affect the decisions they make. Whenever possible, try to learn a person's story and where they came from, because buried there, you might find important clues to what makes them tick.

My wealthy grandparents are the stingiest people I know because they grew up as poor farmers and were taught from a young age to save and reuse everything. Without knowing this about them, it might appear to someone that they are ungenerous and more than a little crazy for reusing Ziplock bags and plastic forks.

*Personal Relevance*

It would never occur to me to blow $95,000 on a 104 inch curved 3D LED TV screen, but I have a buddy who plans to buy one the second he gets his Christmas bonus this year, because his family is very into watching movies together. The purchase has personal relevance to him.

A judge might decide to sentence a first time rapist to a lifetime in prison because the woman the guy raped was the daughter of a woman he got to know between court hearings, had a brief fling with, and believed himself to be falling in love with.

Personal relevance isn't just about doing what you want, however. Personal relevance is a person's belief that their decision counts for something. For example, a person will decide to go and vote for a president when they feel that their vote will actually count toward putting their preferred candidate in office.

Basically, a person will decide to do something if they feel that making that decision is going to make a difference. My buddy will choose to buy his fancy TV because he believes that it will enhance his family movie nights and bonding experiences. A judge will decide to give a rapist life in prison because he believes that it will give him a better chance with the victim's mother.

Decision-making, while seemingly simple, is usually a very complex process involving many factors and variables. Learning about these will give you great insight into how people tick.

# CHAPTER FOUR: PSYCHOLOGY OF MORALITY

Plato has a fair amount to say on the subject of morality. Do people follow a moral code because it brings them good things or the expectation of some kind of societal reward, or do they follow a moral code because it brings them intrinsic pleasure to do so? Is a person who lives by a moral code happier, as some will say, or conflicted and restricted to a life of tedium as others will say? Is following one's conscience a reward in itself?

The easy answer is that everyone is going to see this matter differently. Morality as a whole is very subjective. Where one person will see adultery, another will see love and a new beginning. The more difficult answer is determining where the line is between universality and subjectivism.

Many scientists say that morality and ethics are nothing more than a person's need to make sense of their gut instincts, but whatever it is, humans throughout recorded history have been concerned about the concepts of good an evil and all the shades betwcen. While morality is often seen as tied to religion, it is little more than a set of logical principles that guide behavior and decisions.

Despite the hundreds, and perhaps thousands of religions in the world, societies at large generally tend to follow the same set of moral rules: don't kill people, don't cheat, don't lie, don't steal things, and those who do these things without a good reason deserve to be brought to justice. There are plenty of nuances and exceptions, of course, but understanding how a person feels about morality is another tooth in the key to understanding the human mind and how it ticks.

### *Stages of Moral Development*

Psychologist Jean Piaget is most famous for his work studying child development and defining different stages as they related to certain cognitive abilities, such as the ability to differentiate between the self and the other, the ability to differentiate between right and wrong, and the ability to start to see nuances within a moral code.

Building on Piaget's work, psychologist Lawrence Kohlberg looked specifically at the moral development of people, defining six stages of moral development that a person can progress through as empathy and life experience increase. Kohlberg believed that a person's sense of justice and morality developed throughout the course of a person's entire lifetime.

The stages are meant to categorize how a person justifies their morality and not as a ranking system to judge how moral someone is in relation to others. That means that a person with a higher level of moral development won't necessarily be more moral than one at a lower stage; he or she will merely have the ability to justify their moral perspective with great cognitive complexity.

*Stage One: Obedience and Punishment*

At the obedience and punishment stage of moral development, a person is most concerned with the direct consequences their actions will have on them. For example, a child might believe that stealing cookies from the cookie jar is morally wrong because Mom spanked her for it. She therefore chooses not to steal more cookies, because she doesn't want a spanking, or she is sneakier about stealing the cookies in the future.

While often the people at this stage are children, I've met my fair share of adults still in the obedience and punishment stage. A twenty-two year old guy I used to work with at the bar only bothered to show up to work because he lived with his mom, and she would take away his gaming console if he didn't go work his scheduled shift. He complained about it constantly, not seeming to understand that there were a variety of other reasons why he should go to work, like not leaving his coworkers short-staffed and totally stressed out on a Saturday night after not bothering to call in to say he couldn't make it.

Moral responsibility at stage one is all about avoiding behaviors that bring about negative results.


*Stage Two: Self-Interest*

At stage two, or the self-interest stage, a person starts to ask the question, "What's in it for me?" The person starts to understand that their actions can get them things, and their morality is defined by whatever they believe to be in their own best interests. At stage two, self-interest is defined narrowly without taking into account one's reputation or relationships with groups of people. This person recognizes others only insofar as others will benefit them.

I have a coworker at the office who is stuck at stage two of moral development. I'll call her Doreen. She's perfectly competent at her job and meets the baseline requirements for her yearly raise, but when the boss asks her to take on an extra project that involves doing some financial work for a homeless shelter, her first question is, "Am I getting paid overtime for it?" The boss tells her no, that it's a pro bono case, so she declines to do the extra work, even though taking on the extra project and excelling at it would have advanced her reputation with the company and put her in the running when a promotion opportunity came up.

Since Doreen wasn't able to see beyond the immediate payoff, she judged that the pro bono case wasn't worth her time, regardless of who would have benefited from her expertise.

*Stage Three: Interpersonal Accord and Conformity*

In stage three of moral development, a person is most concerned with conforming to societal expectations of what it means to be moral. People in this stage have begun to recognize the social benefits of being perceived as good, and they seek approval from their community. They want to be liked, and they are aware enough of the feelings of others to understand that behaving in a certain way makes other people like them more.

At stage three, concepts like respect, gratitude, and the golden rule come into play. It also becomes easier to differentiate between actions and intentions.

For example, if, during a game of basketball, someone accidentally smacks his opponent in the face while reaching to intercept the ball, the guy who was smacked, at stage three development, might be more apt to understand when explained that his opponent didn't intend to smack him and let the matter go without returning the favor.

*Stage Four: Authority and Social Order Maintaining*

At stage four, people begin to think beyond strictly what will personally benefit them and begin to see upholding rules, laws, and regulations as a necessary means of upholding a functional society. They will believe that following the rules is a moral necessity and see breaking the rules as immoral, or wrong, because of a central ideal that they hold to. After all, if one person litters, everyone might do it, and then the city parks and streets would fill up with ugly trash that will kill animals and make people sick.

Stage four is where most adults stay in terms of moral development. A lot of my parents' friends, who have lived long, law-abiding lives, have been in this stage of moral development for most of their lives. They drive the speed limit or pay the fines if they don't, remember to renew their car insurance every six months, go to the dentist, show up to their jobs faithfully, teach their kids and grandkids the rules of society, and sleep soundly at night believing that having a good life is as simple as that.

And unless something drastic happens to open their eyes to the nuances of where the laws and rules fail, they will happily remain at this stage. It usually takes an eye opening experience to move beyond this stage, and many first world citizens never have the displeasure of seeing the brokenness of the system they faithfully uphold day in and day out.

*Stage Five: Social Contract*

At stage five of moral development, a person is able to interpret the rules as more of a social contract to be upheld by all parties and eliminated when it ceases to do the greatest amount of good for the greatest number of people. A person at stage five can differentiate between the rules and values of a community versus an individual and believes that individual perspectives on morality should be mutually respected.

A person who views laws and rules as social contracts sees the rules as more fluid than a person in any of the previous stages. Rather than mandates, they are guidelines that generally help society to function, and when they fail to promote the general welfare, they should be thrown out or revised.

The entire democratic method of government is said to be based on a stage five moral complexity. People vote on what they believe to be right and work to eliminate what they believe to be wrong. While in stage four people believe that they have a duty to uphold the law, in stage five they believe that they have a duty to make sure that the laws themselves are moral.

## Stage Six: Universal Ethical Principles

In stage six of moral development, a person subscribes to a set of universal ethical principles that go beyond fear of punishment, self-interest, legality, or a set of rules that a majority of people have agreed on. A person at stage six is most concerned with the justice of any given action or situation. They will follow a law provided they feel that it is grounded in justice, and they feel that they have an obligation to break the law if it fails to uphold justice.

An IRS investigator whose job it is to try to find evidence of tax fraud in a cult community that has registered family homes as churches in order to evade taxation must prove that not all members of the churches are believers in their religion. When the investigator discovers that one woman isn't a believer, she is legally obligated to report her, but when she hears that the woman is afraid to leave the religious community because she knows that the community leader will take her children from her, the investigator instead calls a service for abused women and helps the woman and her children escape from their imprisonment within the cult community.

The investigator, who believed in the universal right to personal freedom over the government mandated duty to not lie on tax forms, acted on her higher sense of universal morality instead of on her legal responsibility to report tax fraud. She knew that reporting the fraud would land the mother in jail and her children in foster care, and she didn't feel that this was just.

While this stage of moral development seems like the epitome of what it means to be moral, it can be equally dangerous when applied by the wrong person.

For example, a murderer might be able to use a similar reasoning to justify his murderous deed. Perhaps he feels that the system has let him down and that he must therefore take justice into his own hands. He killed the man because the man had an affair with his wife, and his wife divorced him and left him with nothing because of a prenuptial agreement he'd signed as a joke back when they were young and in love and couldn't imagine divorcing. The court takes his wife's side at the trial, and, furious, he kills the man who took his wife, his prosperous business, and his happiness with no remorse for his action. He feels that he's merely picked up where the law left off, and he will serve his jail time believing that he is an innocent man.

Stages five and six are where morality and psychology get truly messy. A person at these stages is willing to question things and see the gray areas for what they are—and act on their gut instinct. They can recognize the frailty of humans and the fallibility of the societal rules. Whether these are people smuggling aid to refugees or terrorists, they are acting on beliefs that transcend popular opinion. These are the people for whom the threat of punishment won't deter them from doing what they feel is the right and just thing.

Understanding what stage of moral development a person is at gives you valuable insight into their personal psychology and how they tick, as it can help you predict their responses in situations pertaining to morality and ethics.

# CHAPTER FIVE: PSYCHOLOGY OF PERCEPTION

When I was a kid the neighbor lady accused me of painting the side of her house with graffiti. She swore to my mother that I had skipped class to do it; she had seen me running away with red paint on my clothes. When I came home from school with red paint on my shirt, my parents were livid. The evidence seemed incriminating.

But while all of the clues seemed to point me out as the guilty party, there was one problem; I wasn't the graffiti artist. The red paint on my shirt was from my painting class at school. I'd leaned over my palette to see something my teacher was pointing out on a classmate's artwork and accidentally smeared myself with red paint. I'd tried to wash it out, but it was oil based and only spread and clung harder to the fabric of my shirt.

Despite my feeble explanation about the paint on my shirt, my parents didn't bother to call the school and verify my attendance. Instead, they grounded me for a month for a crime I didn't commit, and even to this day they believe I did it. I never figured out who the real culprit was, but I bet whoever he or she was had a good laugh over the whole situation.

Veracity is usually based on a perception of evidentiary support. If the evidence, gathered through one or more of the five senses, points in one direction, that's the direction people will generally look. A person might flatly deny the evidence, but unless they can give proof of another scenario, then the ones questioning them will stick with what their senses seem to be telling them.

*Seem* is the operative word here. Perception isn't only about the facts that are gathered through the sense. It is also about an individual's interpretation of these facts, and that's where perception starts to feel tricky and out of control, because while you can sometimes control the facts that are presented, the words used to present them, and the order in which they are presented, you aren't in control of the subjective way in which a person will perceive what you are presenting.

A lawyer in a courtroom will work hard to censor the evidence that is allowed into the trial, wanting to present only the evidence that shows their client in the best possible light. She will choose her words carefully to frame a more sympathetic argument. She will behave in a way that she feels will inspire trust in her and her client. But at the end of the trial, she and her client are at the mercy of the jury members' perceptions.

There are two different kinds of perception that I'll be talking about in this chapter. The first is the perception of the senses. You can hear, see, taste, smell, and feel because of the receptors on your body that carry stimuli to the brain. My parents could see the red paint on my shirt. My mother noted my guilty expression. The other kind of perception is more of an extension of the first: how you interpret clues from the rest of your senses. My mother interpreted my guilty face to mean that I'd put graffiti on the neighbor's house rather than that I felt bad about ruining the shirt Mom had just bought for me.

*Perception and What Others Think*

Some might ask, "Why do you care what people think of you?"

My question to them is always, "Why *don't* you care what people think of you? What people think about you is one of the single most important factors in determining where you are able to get in life, who you are able to be friends with, where you are hired to work, how much money you make, and what your marriage and partnership options are, how your children turn out, and, to some extent, whether you are able to maintain happiness." People don't tend to do favors for people they dislike, after all. Kindness is a luxury that most people save for those they either like or pity, and it's hard to pity someone you dislike.

In this world, perception can be everything, and, despite popular talk show hosts telling us to the contrary, most of the population understands that and acts accordingly. Our culture likes to tell us to follow our hearts, to not care what anyone else thinks, but in the same breath, it tells us which clothes to wear, what the most stylish haircut is, and where the best neighborhoods are for raising our families. The world spins on an axis of what others think, and most people will be willing to go to great lengths in order to have others perceive them in a positive light.

When people go out in public to meet new people, they tend to deliberately put their best foot forward. A businesswoman going to a professional conference for networking purposes will dress stylishly, speak in complete sentences and with confidence, and will use her best table manners. A high school kid trying to fit in with the cool kids might fashionably abbreviate words, dress like the others, and be well versed in all of the coolest subjects to talk about.

Because humans are based in communities, it's hard to interpret a perception without input from others. A woman walking down the street might see me and cross to the other side because she perceives that I am a man and a stranger who is big enough, and probably strong enough, to attack her and win. She knows from experience that if a man she thought she cared about could abuse her, then a stranger is certainly capable of the same abuse.

How does she make the leap from big man to dangerous threat? Because she lives in a community of people for which this dangerous threat is real. If I wanted to approach this woman, maybe because I see that as she crosses the street, she accidentally drops something out of her pocket, I need to understand how my approaching her will make her feel—I need to understand how she ticks—in order to contrive the most positive interaction possible.

I could yell at her and run after her, for example, but what would you do if a large man started yelling and chasing you? If you were a small woman, you would probably do your best to get the hell out of dodge. Or I might say, loud enough for her to hear, "Ma'am, you dropped something," and hold it up, while being careful to keep my hands where she can see them, so that I seem less threatening to her. I don't know what kind of experiences she's had, so it's a good idea to be courteous and think about actions as they relate to strangers.

There's a saying that goes, "Who you are in secret is who you really are." I think the same can be said for who a person is in public. You can learn as much about how someone seeks to manipulate perception as you can about who they are when they aren't trying to manipulate public opinion at all. You can learn even more from comparing the two selves to each other.

We've all known or been that person who will go to church on Sunday and act super religious but who will get drunk, sleep around, vandalize public property, and trash other peoples' homes every other day of the week. We call these people hypocrites, and they make for a fascinating study in perception, because some of them are true masters at compartmentalizing their lives such that certain people think they are one person, and certain other people think that they are a totally opposite sort of person.

Things aren't always what they seem. Neither are people. An important step to understanding how people tick is to recognize that what people choose to present of themselves isn't always a definition of who they are. Many will argue that you are what you do. I argue that an action is one facet of a person's identity in the muddle of complexity that is the human condition.

*Perception and Memory*

Memory is a fascinating animal. In a scientific sense, memories are created in an area of the brain called the hippocampus, which develops in early childhood into an instrument that can be used to retrieve memories into adulthood. Since this part of the brain isn't fully developed at the time of birth, it is impossible for a person to have a memory from their first year or two of life.

But that hasn't kept some psychologists from trying to help patients access memories from infancy. Through hypnosis or suggestion, many people have found that they can "remember" scenes from their infancy. Biologically, this is impossible. These are called impossible memories. So are these people lying about their memories?

Memory, it turns out, is easy to tarnish and difficult to verify. In the 80s and 90s, several cases came to light about psychiatrists using hypnosis to help patients remember vivid accounts of childhood abuse and rape by parents, priests, or other people who were close to them.

In one case, the patient believed that her mother held her down while her father raped her many times between the ages of 7 and 14. She remembered becoming pregnant twice and being forced to abort the baby herself with a coat hanger. Her father was a clergyman, and when these accusations came to light, he was forced to resign from his post. When a doctor gave the young woman a medical examination, it was discovered that she was a virgin who had never been pregnant. The psychiatrist was taken to court and sued for $1 million.

This is a very extreme example, but it perfectly illustrates the power of suggestion on memory. By merely suggesting something and asking a person to imagine the scenario in a certain way, false memories can be created and existing memories can be tampered with.

False memories are created by combining real memories with suggestions of the fake memories. As time elapses, the person is likely to dissociate the source of the false information from the information itself and come to believe in the validity of the new, false information.

A more down to earth example of this is a car accident I was in with two of my friends about ten years ago. I was driving home from a party that night. I was the sober driver, and the others were a little bit sloshed. I came to the last intersection before our apartment and turned left at the stop sign. As I was turning, another vehicle ran the stop sign on the opposite side of the intersection and t-boned my car on the passenger side. None of us were hurt, fortunately, but talking about the event years later, our memory of how the accident happened has evolved. My one buddy suggested at one point that the intersection had a stoplight, and we had a protected arrow when the other car hit us. Both of them now stand by that version. I always argue that it was actually a stop sign. I remind them both that they were drunk. They inform me that they were practically sober at that point. We continue to disagree. The one point on which we don't disagree on is that none of us remembers what happened to the other driver after they hit us.

It just goes to show that just because we remember something doesn't mean that it happened. After all, I've woken up from vivid dreams in which I'm making out with Megan Fox feeling that it must have been real, and that is a false memory that I will cherish always.

Does this mean that memory is always untrustworthy? The short answer is yes. There's not yet any scientific way to prove whether a memory is true or false unless quantitative evidence can be gathered and examined to verify it. The longer answer is not necessarily; a person's testimony is still, after all, generally considered to be credible in a court of law. While it must usually be corroborated with physical evidence in order for a charge to stick, human testimony is valued and sought after to win trials.

It also makes up the bedrock of a person's character and helps to determine how they behave and what kinds of decisions they make for themselves. Most people don't deliberately remember things the wrong way. Survival depends on them remembering accurately where the food is, how to protect themselves, how to get out of speeding tickets, what happened last time they were cornered in an alley alone at night, and what the password is to their online banking system. Good memory is good survival in many cases. What is the safest shortcut home at night? How did you purify your drinking water the last time you went camping? What's the greatest number of beers you can have before you start puking?

*Perception and Deliberate Alteration*

People do drugs and drink alcohol in order to alter their perceptions of reality. Even a dose of caffeine in the morning is meant to alter perception by making one feel more alert and open to new sensory experiences.

Perception, sensory and social, are important aspects of human identity, and understanding this is key to figuring out how people tick.

# CHAPTER SIX: PSYCHOLOGY OF BEHAVIOR

A woman walks into a bar. She orders a Shirley Temple and sits in the corner sipping it and nervously looking around her. After half an hour, she checks her watch, visibly takes a deep breath, gets up, and goes into the restroom.

After twenty minutes, she comes out of the restroom clutching her phone in one had. Her eyes are puffy and bloodshot, and she's unsteady on her feet. She dials a number into her phone with shaky fingers and presses the call button. She holds the phone to her ear and waits. Panic mounts behind her eyes as she waits for the first ring, the second ring, the third ring, and then a voicemail. She hangs up without leaving a message. She returns to her table in the corner and sits. Her drink has been cleared in her absence, but she doesn't seem to notice or care.

Her fingers fiddle with a napkin and then start tearing it to shreds as if of their own volition.

As she scans the room, she takes deep breaths: in through her nose, out through her mouth. She seems to be keeping control of herself only barely. She picks up her phone and dials one more time. She waits, but this time the call is picked up right away.

"I can't meet you here tonight," she says. Her brows draw upward in fear. "You're here already? I want out. I can't do it. I think there's something wrong, and..." Her words trail off as her eyes lock on the man standing in front of her.

He clicks his pay as you go flip phone shut with a snap and sits across from her at the table. His back is straight. His shoulders are broad and powerful looking. Something in the way he sits says that he's only sitting down for show; he fully intends to leave with what he came for.

The woman is unable to control her tears. They slide unchecked from her eyes, and she shakes her head at him frantically several times.

He leans in. "If you make a scene here, I will make sure that you never get home to your family ever again. His hand has slipped something cold and metallic from his waistband and pressed it to the inside of the woman's thigh.

She jumps, chokes, and makes a studied effort to contain herself.

He gestures with his head for her to stand, and she does.

I have alerted the bouncers, and they stop him at the door to ask him a series of questions designed to do nothing more than annoy him and stall until the cops get there and disarm him.

His stance as he talks to the bouncers is equal parts cocky and annoyed, and he reluctantly takes out his ID in response to a question of theirs. He'll indulge them, because he's so close to getting away with another victim.

Then he hears the police sirens. They round the corner of the street the bar is on, and he realizes that his number is up. He whips out his gun and trains it on the young woman shaking at his side.

"You let me go before the cops get here, or I will shoot her," he says.

But this isn't the first terrified woman I've seen him with, and I've read up on him. He operates an egg bank, and the women he meets here are egg donors who have been on hormone treatments and are supposed to meet him to have their eggs harvested. The women usually seem afraid of him when they see him, and some have declined to go with him. I initially thought that he might just be some pervert, but now I know better. The long and short of it is, he needs this woman alive, and the bouncers know this. So do the cops.

By the time the cops bust into the bar, most everyone inside are aware that something is going down and are behaving in every manner from totally panicked to craning their necks for a better view.

"We know you won't shoot the girl," one of the bouncers says. But that is a mistake. The man instead points his gun at the bouncer and pulls the trigger. Screams begin to rock the bar, as the Friday night bar hoppers feed off the hysteria those around them, becoming a dangerous roomful of molten panic.

Another shot follows the first, and this time it's the would-be kidnapper who falls. The bouncer is taken away in an ambulance, still alive, somewhat conscious and fortunate that the bullet missed any major organs or arteries.

This night always comes to mind whenever I think about human behavior and what it says about motivations, character, and reactions in particular circumstances. There was something equal parts astonishing and predictable about the whole series of actions that made me feel that I understood the cause and effect nature of behavior a tiny bit better in all the chaos, violence, and adrenaline.

This chapter will focus on behavior and what it can teach you about how the human mind ticks.

The behavioral approach to psychology is the opposite side of the cognitive psychology coin. Behaviorists believe that you can understand a person based on the way they behave. While cognitive psychology tends to take into account genetics and pre existing conditions, behavioral psychologists tend to imagine that we are all born equal—as blank slates waiting to be written on—and entirely the product of our experiences.

While a cognitive psychologist might look into family medical history to see if there is any history of psychosis, a behavioral psychologist will look into an individual's past in order to determine what experiences they've had that might have led to their current behavioral patterns. Both branches of psychology have equally fascinating and useful contributions to make to understanding people and the way their minds tick.

The saying goes, "Actions speak louder than words," and behaviorists agree.

## Behavior and Motivation

Talk is cheap, but taking action always costs a person something, whether that's money, pride, energy, reputation, time, freedom, or any number of other currencies a person may choose to spend.

A person's motivation can be conscious or subconscious. A child in foster care might start badly acting out when she starts to become attached to her foster parents because she's terrified of being abandoned yet again. She might not realize that she's throwing tantrums or stealing things because she's afraid, but that doesn't make her motivation any less real.

People general put about forty hours of their time every week into a job. They sacrifice a large chunk of their time in order to obtain money, which they feel gives them a greater sense of personal security and freedom. Of course, there are some of us who work because we love working and are addicted to that sense of satisfaction that we get from accomplishing a complicated task and making a difference.

From behind the bar, I have an opportunity to watch relational motivations develop between couples on first dates. I can often take a good guess about what their motivations are by the way they carry themselves and the kinds of subjects they choose to talk about. Most of us can intuitively tell what a date's objective is by the way he or she behaves though you might tend to notice a different behavior than I would.

My friend Charlotte, who is fit and attractive, tells me that she can always tell if a guy is wanting a relationship or casual sex by where his eyes go when the conversation lulls. She says that a guy wanting a relationship will make a concentrated effort to be polite in his gaze. "He might look at my boobs," she says, "but he is careful to snap his eyes back to my face as soon as he realizes where he's looking." On the other hand, a guy who just wants to hook up won't make any great effort to train his gaze on her face. His behavior will match his intentions.

As a man, when I'm on a date, I can usually tell what a woman wants from me based on how often she touches me and where. A woman who wants to have sex will tend to touch a guy's arm, ears, face, torso, or anyplace strangers who aren't contemplating sex with each other don't normally touch on purpose.

Behavior tends to coincide with emotions, but you can gain valuable insight in motivation and character when it doesn't. Maybe a father's face is saying he wants to strangle his daughter, but his hands are gently stroking her back. Perhaps she's just accidentally broken a super expensive piece of equipment that he's just paid for, and she feels horrible about it. His gesture doesn't match his anger, perhaps because his anger isn't his primary motivation. Perhaps his love and affection for her overrides his momentary anger at her negligence, and helps him to behave in this seemingly incongruous manner.

People will rarely have only one motivation that they are acting on. How many things can you think of off the top of your head that you want right now? Money, fame, being liked, Netflix, cake, sex, a Ferrari, Megan Fox, a soft blanket, a new computer, a giant TV, a photographic memory, and to know seven languages? Yeah, me too. These wants switch back and forth in levels of importance depending on where I'm at, with whom, and what I'm doing. I'll act on the desire to have any of these when I feel that I have a decent shot at getting it and when it's not overridden by another desire.

A gold digger meets a wealthy man and ends up falling in love with him. What began with a motivation for wealth and status ends in a mash-up of those motivations combined with love and passion. She was attracted to his money initially, but she fell in love because of his character and charming personality. Maybe they get married and seven years later she's also in it for the fashionable designers who will hand tailor all of her clothing and her desire to have a baby, because her husband works all the time, and she's lonely for affection.

This has only given you a taste for what kinds of things motivate behaviors, but if you look around you, watch people, and check out other resources on behavior and psychology, there's a crazy lot of information you can learn in addition to this.

*Behavior and Character*

Behavior, as I have been saying, is a lot more complicated than mere actions. It is often the result of a crushing array of variables—emotion, perception, education, morality, and past decisions. If a woman walks into a bank and robs it while holding the bank teller at gunpoint, she might be living any number of stories. Maybe she loves the thrill of it. Maybe she's desperate, and this is the only thing she can think of to solve her problems with the mob.

While behavior is often a mark of character, it is not the whole expression of it.

Growing up going to Sunday School as a kid, I learned that sometimes you have to do things because they are the right things to do even if you don't feel like it. You have to pay taxes. You have to be kind to elderly widows who are rude to you. You have to honor your parents. You have to give money to charities. I was taught that doing good deeds in spite of not feeling like doing them, could bring about good feelings and make you want to do it more.

Many behaviorists would agree. It's easy for a person do the stuff they want to do or feel like doing, but it's a lot harder to work up the energy to do the stuff they don't want to do. Noting what a person does in spite of feeling tired or reluctant can give you valuable insight into how they tick. The reverse is also true. When you meet a person who is never willing to help out a friend unless he feels like it, you have gained valuable insight into his character. I mean, let's face it, none of us like the hassle of moving, but noble and good friends help friends move, even though it sucks.

On a slightly different note, the content of a person's character doesn't have to line up with how they feel about themselves. For example, according to the Princess Diaries movie (stop judging me), "Courage is not the absence of fear, but the feeling that something else is more important." This is a prevalent theme in many superhero movies as well.

A person doesn't have to feel courageous in order to be courageous. They don't have to feel fast or smart or strong in order to be fast or smart or strong. Feelings are evasive. While they are important, and while they often affect behavior, they don't have to with sufficient motivation or character. Behavior can happen outside of emotions and feelings, which is one more thing that makes the study of psychology fascinating.

# CHAPTER SEVEN: PSYCHOLOGY OF RELATIONSHIPS

In terms of things people depend on the most, relationships are the single most powerful influence in the world. Relationships make the world go round. I'm not just talking about romantic relationships, but all relationships. Parents and children, teachers and students, bartender and customer...

When I work a shift at the bar, I'm always cognizant of the fact that doing my job is about way more than the logistics of which mixer to add to which liquor. It's about making people feel happy and good. I want them to leave my bar feeling better and more relaxed than when they entered it, and I want them to come back. Bars stay open on the basis of relationships. As a bartender, I'm the one listening, giving compliments and recommendations, and showing them that I recognize their worth and humanity. I have seen that when people feel valued and respected, they are more open to having a good time. When they have a good time, they remember, and they tell their friends.

Before a salesman gives his pitch, he'll ask a customer questions in order to build rapport. This relationship-building step is important, because it makes the customer feel more at ease and more likely to make a purchase from that particular salesman.

Everyday relationships are less about saying and doing the right things than they are about the appearance of honesty and good humor. A person can fumble their way through a conversation with a coworker, and if they can laugh at their foibles while still getting their point across, they might still get exactly what they want.

If you take some time to notice people who are great at building instant rapport with people, you will notice that these are not necessarily the smoothest people; they are usually just people good at projecting a sense of trustworthiness.

Many, many things go into the process of relationship development, and literally thousands of books and articles have been written to analyze and explain them. In this chapter, I'll focus on four important aspects of relationship development that I think will give you the best picture of how people tick: proximity, physical attractiveness, similarity, and familiarity.

*Proximity*

Proximity usually refers to geographic closeness. Although one could argue that proximity is less important in the digital age, people generally still prefer to develop relationships with people who live near them.

Proximity is simply the platform through which a person knows someone. Sometimes you know each other because you frequent the same bar every weekend. Maybe you went to school together. Maybe you converse on an anime discussion board. You don't become friends with people you've never met, even if the meeting was virtual. Duh. Proximity allows everything to begin.

*Physical Attractiveness*

Countless studies have been done showing that people tend to perceive attractive people as more likeable and trustworthy than people who are obese, unkempt, or who don't fit whatever the bracket for beauty is at the time. Statistically, beautiful people are perceived to be more healthy, successful, and happy than people who didn't win the genetic lottery. This is probably not helped by the fact that most TV and movie portrayals of smart, happy, successful people are also attractive. The bad guy is inevitably the clownishly ugly man or woman in children's shows, teaching children from a young age that ugly is bad; beautiful is good, in terms of morality.

Naturally, in terms of romance, people want to be with people they find to be sexually attractive. A rampant hookup culture has made physical attractiveness one of the primary requirements for a casual hookup, after willingness. Young people especially are drawn in by the allure of beauty and seek out attractive partners, even if they don't have compatible personalities or beliefs.

We'd like to believe that we're not shallow. We care about things like intelligence and personality, but when we meet someone for the first time, the first things we tend to notice about them relate to their appearance. What are they wearing? Are they physically attractive? Do they look good in those jeans?

Occasionally my bar will host a speed-dating event, because the owner is super into being the hottest place in town to meet that significant other. Working these events, I've gotten to watch a lot of people meet, and there's a real difference between couples who find each other physically attractive and couples where one or both do not find each other to be physically attractive.

The biggest indicator of whether two people will express interest in seeing each other again is whether they found each other to be attractive in the first place. If one of those two people has a great personality, then speed dating is probably not for them.

*Similarity*

Proximity allows a person to meet someone, and physical attractiveness prompts them to walk up and introduce themselves, but similarity is often what keeps them talking. Unless a person is an exceptionally good conversationalist, it's hard to maintain a conversation with someone who has nothing in common with them.

I've been to countless awkward social functions at which I've only known the host and have done my best to mingle and chat and keep talk flowing. One time specifically, I met a woman I thought was attractive and started asking her questions about herself. She said that she was a Wiccan who worked as a dermatologist. It turned out that I knew nothing about either of those subjects, and didn't know what to ask after that. After all, I didn't want to reveal my complete ignorance on the subject or accidentally ask something offensive to her.

Similarity is a kind of social lubricant in many situations. How many times have you been at a party and had nothing to say to someone until you found out that they worked in the same field as you or had the same hobby? Suddenly, you look up, and it's time to leave the party.

When you're learning what makes people tick, don't forget that whatever you are feeling in social situations in which relationship-building is paramount, plenty of other people feel as well. If you're nervous, you're probably not the only one. Is she laughing at the lame joke you just told? She's maybe being polite because she doesn't know what to say either.

A good tip for figuring people out when you're in social situations is to figure out what you have in common with them, as similarities are stepping stones.

While physical attractiveness might determine your likelihood of wanting to see someone again, similarity can foster familiarity and thus liking. You are more likely to like someone who has some things in common with you. That is the reason why there are so many movies and sitcoms in which one or both characters are going out of their way to figure out what their love interest likes so that they can pretend to like the same thing.

*Familiarity*

Repeated exposure to a new thing or person tends to lend, along with familiarity, a sense of liking. This is called mere exposure effect. Mere exposure effect is something you've probably experienced in the instance of seeing a photo of yourself. Because most faces aren't perfectly symmetrical, the photo you see of yourself from your dad's retirement party might look bad or uncomfortable to you, because it is not quite the same image as the face you see in the mirror every day. Your friends will tell you that you look good, and you will insist that you don't. They might be lying to you to preserve your ego, but they probably aren't, because that's the you they see all the time.

Something familiar has a tendency to feel more safe and approachable, which are both contributors to liking someone.

Ultimately, while attractiveness and similarities matter, most people will prefer to be in relationships for the reward of being liked. It's easy to like someone who makes us feel good while we're around them. If a person wants to win a new friend or lover, the best thing they can do in most circumstances is to reward them for being with them by giving compliments and gifts.

A lot of relationship advice books out there advise people to play hard to get, but most people don't want to be strung along and in a constant state of uncertainty about how the other person feels about them. They want to know that they are liked.

On the other hand, familiarity is the reason why bad relationships often recur or continue. Better the devil you know than the one you don't, right? Maybe they're not happy in their current relationship, but at least they know what to expect. There's a certain level of comfort just in that certainty, which is an important thing to remember when your friend keeps going back to her scummy ex. She's not being totally crazy; she's attracted to what is familiar to her, and psychologically speaking, that's a normal thing to feel.

# CONCLUSION: PSYCHOLOGY AND THE POWER OF GOOD

Understanding how peoples' minds work comes with its pitfalls. For one, when you can clearly see a person's motivations and thought processes, there comes a certain responsibility to use your powers of observation and understanding for the betterment of yourself and those around you. For another, not everyone will accept or appreciate your help when you offer it to them, which is frustrating, because in those cases you will feel helpless.

But on the plus side, there will always be someone who needs help and will welcome it from you.

I met my now girlfriend Lena while I was working one of my occasional Saturday night shifts at the bar several years ago. A woman came in with a guy who spent their entire date eyeing the butts on other women. She seemed agitated, because she would say something, and he would say, "What?" as if he hadn't been listening to her. She came up to the bar to grab another whiskey sour, and I stepped out on a limb.

"Your boyfriend is an asshole," I said to her.

She looked surprised. She tried to make her face angry, but I saw the sadness underneath the show of anger. "I don't know what I'm doing wrong," she said.

"You've been trying to engage him in conversation for forty-five minutes, and he's distracted looking at other women. You deserve better."

She didn't look sure too sure about that.

"Look," I said, "I can see that he's not making you happy, and you deserve to be with someone who makes you happy. You should go dump him and then come back over here for a drink on me, and we'll laugh gleefully at your newfound freedom."

So she did.

I saw her a couple of weeks later with another guy. This guy didn't seem much better. He talked over her, made lewd jokes at her expense, and looked at her with microexpressions of contempt. She came up to the bar to refill her drink and asked me what I thought of this guy.

I told her exactly what I saw in his behavior and expressions. It became a weird little routine for us. She would come in with a guy, and after the first round of drinks, I told her what I saw. Sometimes he seemed like a decent guy, and then I wouldn't see her for a few months, but she'd always be back, until she no longer came with a man, but just came to hang with me while I worked.

When you understand how people tick, the world is at your fingertips. After all, there is no weapon more versatile and powerful than the human brain.

# BIBLIOGRAPHY

Dietrich, C. (2010). Decision Making: Factors that Influence Decision Making, Heuristics Used, and Decision Outcomes. Retrieved June 13, 2016, from http://www.inquiriesjournal.com/articles /180/decision-making-factors-that-influence-decision-making-heuristics-used-and-decision-outcomes

Gottman, J. M., & Silver, N. (1999). *The seven principles for making marriage work: A practical guide from the country's foremost relationship expert.* New York, NY: Harmony Books.

Loftus, E. F. (1997, September). Creating False Memories. Retrieved June 13, 2016, from http://faculty.washington.edu/eloftus/Art icles/sciam.htm

Micro Expressions | Facial Expressions | Paul Ekman Group. (2016). Retrieved June 13,

2016, from
http://www.paulekman.com/micro-expressions/

The Myers & Briggs Foundation - MBTI®
Basics. (n.d.). Retrieved June 13, 2016,
from http://www.myersbriggs.org/my-mbti-personality-type/mbti-basics/

Myers, D. G. (2011). *Exploring psychology*. New
York, NY: Worth.

Sleek, S. (2015, September). How Poverty Affects
the Brain and Behavior. Retrieved June
13, 2016, from
http://www.psychologicalscience.org/ind
ex.php/publications/observer/2015/septe
mber-15/how-poverty-affects-the-brain-and-behavior.html